EWI SUPERVISOR'S SKILLS SERIES - VOLUME 1

THE SUPERVISOR'S HR FIX

SUPERVISING WITHIN THE LAW

ESSENTIAL HR COMPLIANCE SKILLS TO LEAD FAIRLY AND PROTECT YOUR TEAM

SHELLY BELL

THE SUPERVISOR'S HR FIX VOLUME 1

SUPERVISING WITHIN THE LAW, ESSENTIAL HR COMPLIANCE SKILLS TO LEAD FAIRLY AND PROTECT YOUR TEAM

BY

Shelly Bell

Copyright © 2025 by Shelly Bell/HRUNeed.LLC. – All rights reserved. It is legal to reproduce, duplicate, or transmit any part of this document in either electronic means or printed format. Recording of this publication is strictly prohibited.

Cover Design: Shelly Bell/ChatGPT (DALL·E)
Illustration: Shelly Bell/ ChatGPT (DALL·E)
Layout: Shelly Bell

ChatGPT (DALL·E) was able to take my thoughts related to the content and create illustrations for the book. This has been a true learning experience for me. I in no way discourage the use of illustrators. But for me this was the most convenient way to produce illustration.

The purpose of copyright is to encourage authors to produce exceptional works that enrich our culture and our open society.

Uploading or disturbing photos, scans or any content from this book without prior permission is theft or the author's intellectual property. Please respect the author's work. Thank you in advance for your support.

Permission Request:
HRUNeed, LLC
shelly.bell@hruneed.com
Atten: Shelly Bell

Dedication

This book is dedicated to: Paul and Sarah Walker

Paul and Sarah Walker were the parents of nine children and a host of grand and great-grandchildren. They both instilled a work ethic and respect for humankind. They were quiet leaders in the community. I can only hope that I can be a fraction of what they demonstrated to me. So, to my parents – I will continue to strive and work for more. Thank you.

Table of Contents

Introduction:...XI
PART I: Supervising Within the Law................1
    Chapter One: FMLA..6
    Chapter Two: FLSA.......................................22
    Chapter Three: EEOC...................................38
PART II: Creating a Workplace of Respect........56
    Chapter Four: Anti-harassment 60
    Chapter Five: Anti-Discrimination..............75
PART III: Safety First – Your Role in a Compliant Workplace..91
    Chapter Six: Safety......................................95
    Chapter Seven: OSHA................................108
Conclusion..127
References..132
Index...136
Acknowledgments.......................................140
About the Author...142

Introduction

First, let me congratulate you on taking the time to invest in your leadership skills. If you're holding this book, you're already a step ahead of many supervisors—you're actively seeking the tools to lead with confidence, protect your team, and stay on the right side of the law.

This book is more than just HR policies. It's about giving you the knowledge and strategies to handle the challenges that land on your desk every single day. Whether you're managing schedules, approving time off, or dealing with a sensitive complaint, the decisions you make carry real consequences—both for your team and your organization.

Here's the problem most supervisors face: you're promoted for your skills, performance, or leadership potential—but not necessarily trained on the HR side of the job. No one tells you that you'll become the first responder to workplace issues, the gatekeeper of compliance, and the daily face of the company's policy. Without the proper knowledge, even well-intentioned supervisors can make mistakes that lead to costly errors, damaged trust, or legal trouble.

That's where this book comes in. Inside, we'll cover six of the most critical areas you'll encoun lines. I still remember a new supervisor who told me, "I just want to manage my people and get the work done—HR makes things too complicated." By the end of his first week, he'd accidentally approved unauthorized overtime, mishandled a medical leave request, and ignored a harassment complaint. Not because he didn't care—but because no one explained the rules to him. After we worked together, he told me, "I had no idea how much of my job was really HR."

This book exists so you don't have to learn those lessons the hard way.

The benefits are clear:

You will:

- Gain confidence in making decisions that protect your team and your organization.
- Know how to spot and address problems before they escalate.
- Improve trust, morale, and respect within your team.
- Avoid costly mistakes that can hurt both people and profits.

Supervisors who've applied these principles tell me they not only sleep better at night—they've seen their teams become stronger, more engaged, and more productive. The difference isn't magic; it's simply having the right tools.

So, let's get started. The chapters ahead will give you the knowledge and practical steps you need to handle HR responsibilities with confidence, fairness, and professionalism. Read on—your team, your company, and your future self will thank you.

Figure 1. Supervising within the law *(original illustration created by Shelly Bell).*

Part 1: Supervising Within the Law

As a supervisor, your role isn't just about leading people—it's about leading them **within the boundaries of the law**. Every decision you make – from approving a timesheet to responding to a leave request – has the potential to impact your team, your company, and your career. Understanding the legal framework that governs the workplace isn't optional—it's essential.

In this part of the book, we'll focus on three critical pillars of HR compliance: **FMLA, FLSA, and EEOC**. Together, these laws form the foundation for how employees are treated, paid, and protected in the workplace.

- **FMLA (Family and Medical Leave Act)** ensures that eligible employees can take protected leave for qualified family or medical reasons without fear of losing their jobs. As a supervisor, your role is to recognize potential FMLA situations early and respond in compliance with the law.

- **FLSA (Fair Labor Standards Act)** sets standards for minimum wage, overtime pay, recordkeeping, and youth employment. Understanding FLSA helps you avoid costly payroll mistakes and ensures fairness in how employees are compensated.

- **EEOC (Equal Employment Opportunity Commission)** enforces federal laws against workplace discrimination. Your decisions in hiring, promoting, and disciplining directly impact compliance and workplace equity.

From an HR Manager's perspective, I can tell you that supervisors are often the **first line of defense** in these areas. You are the eyes and ears of the organization—spotting potential compliance issues before they escalate and setting the tone for how policies are enforced. The problem is that most supervisors don't receive enough practical training on these laws before stepping into the role. That's why this section is here: to give supervisors the **clarity, confidence, and actionable steps** to supervise effectively and legally.

Each chapter will break down the law into plain language, highlight real-world scenarios you're likely to face, and give you strategies to handle them correctly. You'll see what to do, what not to do, and how to partner with HR to keep your team compliant and productive.

Supervising within the law isn't about being overly cautious or letting rules slow you down—it's about protecting your team, your company, and yourself while leading with integrity. When you understand these core laws, you will not only avoid costly mistakes, but also earn the trust and respect of your employees.

By the end of this section, you'll be able to navigate FMLA requests with confidence, apply FLSA rules accurately, and make decisions that align with EEOC standards. This is your legal leadership foundation—one that will support every decision you make as a supervisor.

Chapter One FMLA Compliance

Understanding FMLA – Family and Medical Leave Act

"The strength of a leader lies in their ability to balance performance with compassion." – **Sheryl Sandberg**

Let's start with something you'll probably face as a supervisor sooner than later: an employee dealing with a family emergency or a serious illness. When that happens, your first instinct should be empathy—but your next move must be rooted in compliance. That's where the Family and Medical Leave Act (FMLA) comes in.

FMLA is a federal law that gives eligible employees up to 12 weeks of unpaid, job-protected leave for qualified family and medical reasons. It also ensures that group health benefits are continued during the leave period. Now, you're not expected to know every detail—that's HR's job—but you do need to recognize when a situation might qualify.

Here's the thing: if an employee shares that they're pregnant, adopting, caring for a sick parent, or managing a serious health issue, don't ignore it. Those are triggers. Your job isn't to evaluate whether they **qualify**—it's to point them in the right direction quickly and support them along the way (DOL, 2022; Budd, 2020).

The Family and Medical Leave Act (FMLA), enacted in 1993, is a foundational federal law that allows eligible employees to take up to 12 weeks of unpaid, job-protected leave per year. This law is designed to help employees balance work with significant family or medical issues while maintaining job security. For supervisors, it's essential not only to understand the basics of FMLA but also to support employees with compassion and neutrality.

To be eligible, employees must have worked for their employer for at least 12 months and logged at least 1,250 hours in the previous 12 months. In addition, the employer must have 50 or more employees within a 75-mile radius. Leave can be taken for a variety of reasons, including: the birth or adoption of a child, caring for an immediate family member with a serious health condition, the employee's own serious health condition, or exigencies arising from a family member's military service.

> *"Your employees are your company's greatest asset. Treat them like it."* – **Richard Branson**

As a supervisor, you are not expected to be a legal expert, but you must be able to identify potential FMLA situations and guide employees to HR. Phrases like 'I need time off for surgery' or 'I'm caring for my sick child' are potential FMLA triggers. It's critical to respond empathetically, ensure confidentiality, and immediately refer the employee to HR or the third-party administrator.

According to the U.S. Department of Labor, approximately 20 million workers take FMLA leave annually. Despite this, more than 40% of eligible employees are unaware of their rights under the law.

Employees can also take intermittent leave — short blocks of time off for treatment or chronic conditions. This can be challenging for supervisors managing schedules, but employees must be accommodated without retaliation. Tracking and documentation should be coordinated with HR, not managed informally or publicly.

It is illegal to retaliate against employees for requesting or taking FMLA leave. Actions such as reducing hours, excluding them from meetings, or treating them differently upon return can be considered retaliatory. All return-to-work transitions should be handled smoothly, ensuring the employee is restored to the same or equivalent role.

Legal and Supervisory Responsibilities

As a supervisor, you are more than a leader of day-to-day operations; you are a frontline representative of your organization's compliance obligations. When it comes to the Family and Medical Leave Act (FMLA), your actions—or inactions—carry real consequences. If you fail to recognize a potential FMLA request, delay reporting it to Human Resources, or mishandle the process, you could be contributing to a violation of federal law.

While ultimate legal responsibility rests with the employer, supervisors can be **personally named in legal complaints** if their behavior or decisions are deemed to have interfered with an employee's FMLA rights. This risk is not hypothetical—there have been cases where managers faced personal liability for ignoring qualifying leave requests, making retaliatory comments, or failing to maintain confidentiality.

Your role is not to interpret the law in full detail; that is the responsibility of HR and legal counsel. However, you are **required** to:

- Recognize possible FMLA triggers.
- Respond professionally and without bias.

- Maintain complete confidentiality.
- Immediately refer the matter to HR or your organization's leave administrator
- Document conversations factually and accurately.

Failure to meet these responsibilities can lead to lawsuits, government investigations, reputational damage to the company, and the erosion of trust within your team.

Handling FMLA requests correctly is not just a compliance requirement; it's a leadership duty that protects both your employees and your organization.

Key Takeaway: The Weight and Responsibility of Leadership

As a supervisor, you are more than a task manager; you are a daily representative of your organization's values, culture, and legal responsibility. Your decisions, conversations, and actions directly impact employees' trust in the company, as well as its compliance standing. When it comes to the **Family and Medical Leave Act (FMLA)**, even unintentional missteps—such as delaying a referral to HR, asking the wrong question, or incorrectly documenting leave—can expose your organization (and you) to liability.

That's why it's essential to lead with care, accuracy, and consistency. You don't need to have all the answers, but you do need to recognize when to act, when to refer, and how to maintain confidentiality. Your role is not to interpret the law; that's what your Human Resources team is here for. However, your responsibility is to be alert, empathetic, and professional in your response.

Remember: You're not alone. HR is your partner. Whether you're unsure how to document a leave-related conversation, need guidance on communicating with your team, or simply want to double-check a step in the process—reach out. It's not a sign of weakness; it's a sign of leadership.

When you handle FMLA requests with respect, compliance, and humanity, you foster a workplace culture where employees feel seen, supported, and secure—even during life's most challenging moments. That kind of leadership goes a long way.

Any of these missteps could create legal risk or cause a breakdown in trust.

Glossary Terms	Definition
Equivalent Position	A job that is virtually identical to the original job in terms of pay, benefits, and working conditions.
FMLA	Refers to the Family and Medical Leave Act, a federal law providing eligible employees with job-protected leave for specific family and medical reasons.
Eligible Employee	An employee who meets certain criteria, including working for a covered employer for a specific duration and hours, and working at a location with a certain number of employees within a given radius.
Covered Employer	An employer that is subject to the FMLA, such as public agencies, schools, and private-sector employers with a certain number of employees.
Serious Health Condition	An illness, injury, or condition requiring inpatient care or ongoing treatment by a healthcare provider. This includes overnight hospital stays, chronic conditions, pregnancy, and conditions causing incapacitation for more than three days with continued medical treatment.
Incapacity	The inability to perform regular daily activities, including work or school, due to a serious health condition or its treatment.
Family Member (FMLA)	For FMLA purposes, this typically includes a spouse, son or daughter (under 18 or incapable of self-care due to disability), or a parent.
In Loco Parentis	A relationship where an individual assumes the responsibilities of a parent to a child.

Glossary Terms	Definition
Intermittent Leave	FMLA leave taken in separate periods for a single qualifying reason.
Reduced Schedule Leave	Leave that decreases the employee's usual working hours per week or day due to a serious health condition.
Qualifying Reasons for FMLA Leave	Specific situations allowing an eligible employee to take FMLA leave, such as: 1. Birth, adoption, or foster care placement of a child, and bonding. 2. Caring for a spouse, child, or parent with a serious health condition. 3. The employee's own serious health condition preventing them from performing their job. 4. Reasons related to a family member's military service, including leave for qualifying exigencies due to foreign deployment or leave to care for a servicemember or veteran with a serious injury or illness.
12-Month Period	The timeframe during which an employee can take FMLA leave. Employers can define this period in various ways, such as a calendar year or a rolling 12-month period.
Job Protection/ Reinstatement	The right of an employee returning from FMLA leave to be restored to their original job or an equivalent with similar pay, benefits, and employment terms.

Understanding terms related to the topic of FMLA is a part of the foundation for supervisors in their role. This is why they must know and use them correctly.

Supervisor Tip: Keep FMLA paperwork and conversations strictly confidential. Never leave documents out in the open or discuss leave details with coworkers.

The role of the supervisor includes staying neutral, being informed, and maintaining a professional boundary. It's never appropriate to ask about the details of a diagnosis or treatment plan. Leave all medical verifications to HR or the plan administrator for consideration.

Figure 2. Supervisor Tip: FMLA *(original illustration created by Shelly Bell)*.

Case Study:

Renee, a customer service lead, informs her supervisor that she needs surgery and will be out for four weeks. The supervisor, frustrated with short staffing, says, 'You've already taken a lot of time off.' Renee reports the comment to HR. Though her leave is approved, her performance review later notes her 'frequent absences".'' HR investigates and finds that her absences were protected by FMLA. The supervisor's poor handling results in a written warning and retraining.

_____
_____
_____
_____
_____
_____

Activity:

1. Supervisor FMLA Scenarios
Instructions: Read each statement below and identify whether it might be a trigger for FMLA. Then write how you, as a supervisor, should respond.

1. An employee says they need time off for physical therapy after a car accident.

_____
_____

_____
_____
_____

2. An employee tells you their parent has been hospitalized.

_____
_____
_____
_____
_____

3. An employee shares they're adopting a child in two months.

_____
_____
_____
_____
_____

4. An employee says they feel overwhelmed and need a break, but would not explain further.

_____
_____
_____
_____
_____

2. Supervisor FMLA Scenario

Let's say Marcus, one of your team members, tells you he just found out his wife has been diagnosed with a serious illness. He's unsure of what to do next.

What would you say?

_____
_____
_____
_____
_____
_____
_____

What you should you say.:

1. "Marcus, I'm really sorry to hear that. I want you to know we're here to support you. There may be options available through FMLA that can help. Let's get HR involved today to talk through the next steps."

2. Then, document the conversation factually (date, time, summary), and follow up to make sure HR connected with him. These extra few minutes on your part mean a lot—to Marcus, and to compliance.

FMLA Eligibility Quick Guide

To qualify for FMLA, an employee must:
- Work for a covered employer (50+ employees within 75 miles)
- Have worked for the employer for at least 12 months (not necessarily consecutive).
- Have logged at least 1,250 hours in the past 12 months.

Covered leave reasons include:
- Birth or adoption of a child
  - Caring for a spouse, parent, or child with a serious health condition.
- The employee's own serious health condition.
- Military caregiver or exigency leave.

Figure 3. Quick Guide: FMLA *(original illustration created by Shelly Bell).*

What Not to Do
- Don't ask for medical details.
- Don't express frustration about their absence.
- Don't gossip or speculate with peers.
- Don't delay your response.

Figure 4. Do Not: FMLA (original illustration created by Shelly Bell).

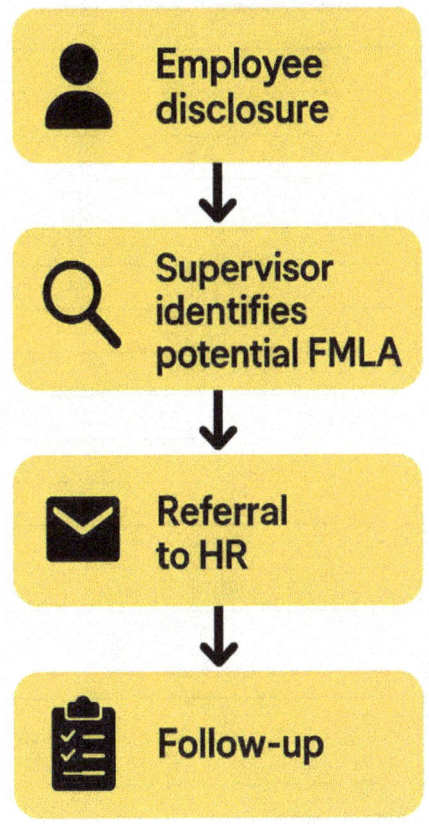

Figure 5. Flowchart: FMLA *(original illustration created by Shelly Bell).*

Notes:

Chapter Two Basics of HR for Supervisors When Dealing with FLSA

"The greatest threat to compliance is assuming someone else is handling it." — **Unknown**

Introduction: Why This Matters to You

As a supervisor, whether you've been leading teams for years or just stepped into your role—you carry a responsibility that goes beyond managing people. You are a gatekeeper for compliance.

The Fair Labor Standards Act (FLSA) might seem like an HR or payroll function, but in reality, your decisions, actions, and even your silence can expose your organization—and you personally—to serious consequences. If you're new to the role, it's easy to overlook these complexities while focusing on team morale or production goals. But trust me: understanding wage and hour rules will serve you well.

*The U.S. Department of Labor recovered over **$213 million** in back wages for more than **150,000 workers** in 2022 alone due to FLSA violations. (U.S. Department of Labor, 2023)*

What is FLSA and Why Should You Care?

The FLSA is a federal labor law that protects employees' rights to fair pay, limits child labor, and mandates overtime eligibility. It defines how employees are classified and how much they must be paid. The law is enforced by the U.S. Department of Labor (DOL), and violations can result in hefty fines and public audits. Supervisors are often considered 'employers' under this law because of their control over work schedules, pay practices, and job duties (Hunton Andrews Kurth LLP, 2023).

> *"**Compliance** isn't about catching mistakes—it's about preventing them."* — **Compliance Week, 2021**

Exempt vs. Non-Exempt: Get It Right

The classification of exempt vs. non-exempt employees determines whether someone qualifies for overtime. Non-exempt employees must receive overtime pay (1.5 x regular rate) for all hours worked beyond 40 in a week. Exempt employees do not—but only if they meet strict requirements related to salary level, salary basis, and job duties. Misclassification is one of the most common FLSA violations. Always check with HR before labeling anyone as exempt.

"When in doubt, record the time. You'll never be penalized for being too accurate." — **HR Professional's Rule of Thumb**

Common Pitfalls for New Supervisors

If you're new to supervising, one of the biggest traps is unintentionally allowing off-the-clock work. Maybe you ask an employee to 'jump on email really quick' after their shift, or you forget to review timecards at the end of the week. Minor oversights like these can snowball into massive liabilities. New supervisors also tend to overlook 'break' policies. An employee who skips lunch to catch up on work must still be paid for that time. It's your duty to ensure these moments are properly tracked and compensated (Department of Labor, 2019).

> *"Leadership is not just about performance; it's about integrity in the process."* — ***Anonymous***

The Role You Play in Timekeeping

You're more than a people manager—you're a process manager. Ensuring time is recorded accurately is your legal responsibility. Even if you didn't personally instruct someone to stay late, if you're aware they did, it must be recorded. Modern timekeeping systems help, but they require your daily oversight. Don't assume HR will catch the errors you miss.

How Veteran Supervisors Get Caught

Even experienced managers fall into habits that violate FLSA. Some assume long-time team members know how to log time correctly, only to find those employees have been skipping documentation on setup or cleanup tasks. Others allow a culture of 'getting it done' without realizing it leads to hours of untracked work. Auditors won't care that you didn't know—it's still your responsibility.

"People don't leave jobs—they leave unfair systems." — Adapted from Gallup Management Study

Unauthorized Overtime: What You Must Do

Many supervisors believe that if overtime isn't pre-approved, it doesn't need to be paid. That is false. Under the FLSA, any time worked must be paid, regardless of whether you authorized it. Your remedy is not to withhold pay—it's to coach the employee or apply discipline per your policy (Ross, 2019).

Supervisors who complete FLSA-focused training **reduce department-level violations by up to 45%** *in the first 6 months of post-training. (Loafman et al., 2024)*

Learning from Devon's Mistake

Devon, a well-meaning warehouse lead, told his team to prep equipment 15 minutes before their shift each morning. Over time, this added up to hundreds of hours of unpaid work. When an employee anonymously reported it, the DOL got involved. The company was forced to pay back wages and fines, and Devon received a formal warning. This wasn't malicious, just untrained leadership. Don't be a Devon. Ask yourself if all the hours worked are truly being recorded.

Model the Behavior

Set the tone. Don't rush employees through breaks. Don't joke about staying late 'off the clock.' Your team will follow your lead. Create a culture of compliance by practicing it yourself. Your credibility and their trust depend on it.

83% of violations *identified during WHD audits (Wage and Hour Division) involve **overtime or misclassification errors**, commonly triggered by inconsistent supervisor practices. (Department of Labor, 2019)*

Checklist for Supervisors – Staying FLSA Compliant

- Review employee classifications annually
- Ensure timekeeping systems are used daily
- Pay for all hours worked—even if unauthorized
- Document time edits with explanations
- Never average hours over two weeks
- Do not require skipped breaks
- Coordinate with HR on policy questions

60% of employees *who experience wage violations report a decline in trust toward their direct supervisor. (Hammer et al., 2019)*

Final Thoughts: Lead with Compliance, Not Consequence

Whether you're stepping into your first supervisory role or have decades of experience leading teams, FLSA compliance is not something you can afford to overlook—or delegate entirely to HR. Your role as a supervisor places you on the front lines of wage and hour law enforcement. Every decision you make about timekeeping, scheduling, and job duties has the potential to protect or jeopardize your team, your company, and yes—your own professional credibility.

Compliance is not about bureaucracy—it's about integrity. The Fair Labor Standards Act was designed to ensure that workers are paid fairly and treated with respect. When you disregard even small FLSA requirements, it sends a message that shortcuts are acceptable. But when you lead with accountability, you build a workplace culture rooted in fairness and trust.

Consider this: FLSA violations don't typically result from major scandals. They stem from "small" things—like failing to record prep time, letting someone skip a break, or misclassifying a team member to avoid overtime. These issues grow quietly in the background until an audit, lawsuit, or employee complaint brings them into full view.

The compliance risks aren't abstract. As the law evolves, courts have increasingly ruled that supervisors and front-line leaders can be held **personally liable** for knowingly ignoring FLSA protections (Hunton Andrews Kurth LLP, 2023). If your name appears on a timecard approval, a performance directive, or an email trail confirming unpaid work—you may be the one answering for it.

So don't wait for HR to "flag something." Don't assume someone else is watching. Be the supervisor who catches it early, asks questions, and models what 'right' looks like. Take initiative to:

- Review classifications regularly.

- Train leads and shift coordinators on proper tracking.

- Intervene when off-the-clock work is suspected.

- Reinforce that overtime must be paid—regardless of approval status.

Being FLSA-compliant is not just a task, it's a leadership responsibility. It reflects your respect for the people who report to you and your commitment to protecting the business.

Truth is, when employees trust that their time is valued and fairly compensated, they stay engaged, loyal, and productive. And when auditors or senior leaders look at your area, they'll see a supervisor who leads with diligence—not damage control.

Glossary Terms	Definition
FLSA (Fair Labor Standards Act)	A federal law that establishes minimum wage, overtime pay eligibility, recordkeeping, and child labor standards for employees in the U.S.
Exempt Employee	An employee who is not entitled to overtime pay due to meeting specific criteria related to job duties, salary level, and salary basis.
Non-Exempt Employee	An employee who is entitled to overtime pay (1.5x) for all hours worked over 40 in a workweek. Usually paid hourly.
Salary Basis Test	One of three tests to determine exemption status. The employee must receive a fixed salary that is not subject to reduction based on the quality or quantity of work.
Off-the-Clock Work	Any work performed by a non-exempt employee that is not properly recorded or compensated, such as checking emails after hours or prepping before a shift.

Lead with knowledge. Act with integrity. Supevise with compliance.

That's how you protect your team — and yourself.

For supervisors, understanding the differences between salaried and hourly employees is essential. Clear distinctions help prevent confusion and ensure responsibilities remain appropriately defined. Mastering these terms is a critical part of your leadership toolbox.

Supervisor Tips

1. **Never assume an employee is exempt based on title.** Always confirm with HR before classifying or reclassifying roles.

2. **Document everything, especially time edits.** Clear notes protect you and the employee in the event of an audit.

3. **Model proper break usage.** If you rush through your lunch, your team will think they have to, as well.

4. **Review timecards weekly.** Spot missed punches, odd hours, or overtime trends early.

5. **Coach behaviors, not time worked.** If someone exceeds hours without permission, address the policy—not the pay.

Figure 6. Supervisor's Tip: Exempt/Non-Exempt *(original illustration created by Shelly Bell)*.

Case Studies

Case Study 1: "Email After Hours"

Scenario: Maria, a non-exempt administrative assistant, regularly responds to emails at night from home. Her supervisor, James, praises her dedication but does not ask her to log this time.

_____
_____
_____
_____
_____

Outcome: After a colleague files a complaint, an internal audit finds 37 hours of unrecorded labor over two months. HR requires retroactive payment, and James is retrained on timekeeping compliance.

Lesson: Praise doesn't replace pay. All hours worked must be logged—even when remote.

Scenario 1: "Just Helping Out"

Jessica, a non-exempt receptionist, tells you she likes to come in 20 minutes early to "warm up the front desk" before the official open. You notice she often begins answering phones and prepping coffee before clocking in.

Discussion Prompt:
How do you approach Jessica? What do you say? How do you correct this moving forward?

_____
_____
_____
_____

Scenario 2: "Pushback on Overtime Pay"

Your peer in another department refuses to approve overtime for a non-exempt employee who worked through lunch and stayed 30 minutes late to cover an emergency. They argue the employee didn't get permission first.

Discussion Prompt:
What is your responsibility? How do you advocate for compliance while respecting peer relationships?

_____
_____
_____
_____

Quick Guide: Supervisor Responsibilities for FLSA Compliance

Do	Don't
Confirm employee classifications with HR	Assume job title equals exempt status
Review timecards weekly	Approve or ignore skipped breaks
Pay for all hours worked (even unauthorized)	Withhold overtime pay due to lack of approval
Train team leads on proper timekeeping	Encourage early starts or late work without pay
Report FLSA concerns to HR promptly	Average hours over multiple weeks to avoid OT

What Not to Do (Supervisor Pitfalls to Avoid)

Don't Do This	Why It's a Problem
Ignore employees who start early or stay late off the clock	This is considered compensable time under FLSA and must be tracked and paid
Approve timecards without reviewing them	Missed punches, skipped breaks, and unrecorded overtime will go unnoticed
Tell employees to "just take care of it later" without proper logging	Creates a culture of undocumented and unpaid work
Assume salaried = exempt	Classification must meet all three exemption tests: salary basis, salary level, and duties
Average hours across two weeks to avoid overtime	FLSA requires weekly accounting, not biweekly averaging
Discourage logging short post-shift tasks	Even five minutes of work must be paid and recorded
Let team leaders create their own timekeeping rules	This leads to inconsistent applications and possible legal exposure

Don't Do This	Why It's a Problem
Delay correcting time-keeping errors	Waiting may cause irreversible audit risk or delayed back pay liability
Allow employees to waive overtime or breaks voluntarily	Rights under FLSA cannot be waived by employees or employers
Assume HR or Payroll will catch compliance issues	As a supervisor, you are the first and most visible point of responsibility

Figure 7. Supervisor's Tips: FSLA *(original illustration created by Shelly Bell)*.

Notes:

Chapter Three Basics of HR for Supervisors When Dealing with EEOC

"Doing the right thing is not the problem. Knowing what the right thing is, that's the challenge." – **Lyndon B. Johnson**

As a supervisor, your role is not just about hitting performance metrics—it's also about creating a work environment where fairness, compliance, and respect thrive. Understanding your responsibilities under the Equal Employment Opportunity Commision(EEOC) isn't a suggestion—it's a necessity for your success.

What is the EEOC and Why Should You Care? The EEOC enforces laws that protect workers from discrimination based on race, color, religion, sex (including sexual orientation and gender identity), national origin, age (40 or older), disability, and genetic information. These laws include Title VII of the Civil

Rights Act (1964), the Americans with Disabilities Act (ADA), the Age Discrimination in Employment Act (ADEA), and the Equal Pay Act.

As a supervisor, you have front-line accountability for ensuring that the workplace reflects those protections. This means you must consider compliance in every decision—hiring, firing, promotions, assignments, and evaluations. One poor decision, even if unintentional, can lead to an investigation.

In my role as an HR Manager, EEOC incidents required a great deal of time. I also understood the possible replication if everything was not done according to federal and state regulations. Documentation, follow-up, and consistent processes saved our organization time and costly consequences.

> *"Fairness is not an attitude. It's a professional skill that must be developed and exercised."* – **Brit Hume**

The Supervisor's Legal Burden

Supervisors are often unaware that they can be held individually liable for certain employment decisions. As highlighted by Hunton Andrews Kurth LLP (2023), courts have increasingly allowed suits against individual supervisors who play a substantial role in discriminatory acts, especially under FLSA and related statutes. That means **YOU** could be named in an EEOC complaint—not just your organization in the case.

In FY 2023, the EEOC received over 73,000 workplace discrimination complaints. The most cited issue? Retaliation. This was followed closely by disability and race discrimination (U.S. EEOC, 2023).

Retaliation: A Common (and Avoidable) Trap

You may feel defensive when an employee makes a complaint—especially if you feel it's unfair or untrue. However, any adverse reaction—like changing their shift, excluding them from meetings, or documenting their errors more harshly—**could be viewed as retaliation.**

According to the National Employment Law Project (2021), retaliation claims are among the easiest to substantiate because they often follow a clear timeline: complaint, then consequence.

> *"Leadership is not about being in charge. It is about taking care of those in your charge."* – **Simon Sinek**

When in doubt, stop and ask yourself:

- Is my response consistent with how I treat others?
- Can I defend this decision with written documentation?
- Have I consulted HR before taking this step?

TIP: Always thank the employee for bringing

concerns forward. Document what they say and immediately escalate it. Do not attempt to "solve" it alone. Your HR Department is here to support you onsite as well as at the corporate level.

Microaggressions and Bias—What You May Be Missing

Many discriminatory behaviors aren't loud—they're subtle. Microaggressions, passive exclusion, and unconscious bias can quietly create toxic and unlawful environments.

Hammer et al. (2019) found that training supervisors to recognize and reduce unconscious bias improves organizational performance and compliance. From skipping certain employees for high-visibility tasks to cracking inappropriate jokes, the tone you set as a supervisor matters. Don't allow shop talk in any form in your department.

Your responsibilities include:

- Rotating responsibilities fairly
- Celebrating inclusive holidays or team milestones
- Listening to feedback about exclusion or unfair treatment
- Avoiding assumptions about roles, abilities, or intent

ADA and FMLA: When Laws Overlap

The Americans with Disabilities Act (ADA) and the Family and Medical Leave Act (FMLA) frequently overlap. For example, an employee recovering from surgery may qualify under both acts—for medical leave and as a person with a disability requiring accommodations.

According to the Department of Labor (2019), understanding the interaction between FMLA and ADA is critical in order to prevent unintentional violations. Supervisors must never penalize employees for using protected leave—even indirectly in performance reviews.

Krieg DeVault (2024) advises adjusting performance metrics and schedules when evaluating employees on leave. It's not about special treatment, it's about legal compliance.

Real-World Tip: If an employee requests help due to a medical issue, never guess at what's needed. Document the request and refer it immediately to HR. You are not expected to determine what's "reasonable."

"You can't lead the people if you don't love the people." – **Cornel West**

Let's complete this exercise to see what you will do.

Case Study: Jasmine's Promotion Denials Incident

Jasmine, a high-performing Latina employee, has been passed over for promotion three times. Her supervisor offers vague reasoning—"not leadership material"—despite her strong evaluations. She is filing an EEOC complaint. The investigation uncovers a pattern: multiple minority women were similarly overlooked for positions within the department.

The company settles the claim, provides back pay, and initiates mandatory supervisor bias training for employees.

Supervisor Misstep: Failure to use objective criteria, resulting in inconsistent documentation and treatment

Lesson for You: Use measurable, documented criteria for promotion and performance reviews. Be able to explain your decisions in writing with supporting facts.

Common Mistakes Supervisors Make

1. Inconsistent discipline – Failing to discipline similarly situated employees equally

2. **Subjective evaluations** –Using phrases like "poor attitude" without defining behavior
3. **Delayed documentation** – Waiting until a problem escalates to start writing things down.

4. **Overconfidence** – Assuming your intentions protect you from liability

What Not to Do:

- Do not dismiss complaints without documentation.
- Do not discuss an employee's complaint with peer
- Do not promise an outcome before investigation.
- Do not forget to follow up with HR.

Handling Complaints the Right Way

When a complaint comes to you:
1. **Thank them** – Always validate the courage it takes to speak up.
2. **Document it** – Write down what you heard, when, and what you did.
3. **Escalate** – Immediately involve HR or the appropriate compliance contact.
4. **Maintain confidentiality** – Only share on a need-to-know basis.
5. **Avoid retaliation** – Don't treat the employee differently in tone, tasks, or attention.

New Insight: Loafman et al. (2024) argue that harmonizing federal anti-discrimination standards means even well-intentioned supervisors must become more aware of multilayered legal exposure—especially in hybrid and decentralized workplaces.

Incorporating Compliance into Leadership Style

You don't need to fear the EEOC. You just need to stay alert, consistent, and proactive.

- Use interview guides to avoid asking illegal questions
- Set clear, written performance expectations
- Keep track of coaching conversations
- Stay up-to-date on protected classes and accommodations
- Ask HR for training—even before there's a problem

Supervisors who focus on people—not just productivity—build stronger, more resilient teams.

Final Thoughts: Lead with Fairness and Precision

Whether you're brand new or a seasoned supervisor, taking time to understand EEOC requirements ensures you protect your team, your company, and yourself. In my experience, documentation and accountability make a significant difference—not just in outcomes, but in employee trust they have for supervisor.

Supervisors shape company culture more than any other role. You're the first line of defense against workplace discrimination. Your leadership directly affects whether employees feel safe, respected, and are treated fairly within an organization or not.

Don't wait for an **audit** or a claim to take this seriously. Lead with intention, integrity, and informed action.

Note: In Compliance, Federal and State Laws are subject to change. Please ensure that you are up to date on any changes that may occur.

Glossary Terms	Definition
EEOC	Equal Employment Opportunity Commission – the federal agency enforcing laws against workplace discrimination.
Retaliation	Adverse action taken against an employee for engaging in a protected activity, such as reporting discrimination or participating in an investigation.
Unconscious Bias	Attitudes or stereotypes that affect understanding, actions, and decisions in an unconscious manner, often influencing workplace behavior.
Reasonable Accommodations	Modifications or adjustments to a job or work environment that enable a qualified individual with a disability to perform essential job functions.
Protected Class	A group of people legally protected from employment discrimination by law (e.g., race, age, gender, disability, etc.).

"Keep in mind that terms and regulations are constantly evolving. Never assume that a law or policy remains the same — always verify the most current requirements."

Supervisor Tips

1. **Document Immediately**: Every conversation related to performance, accommodations, or complaints should be documented factually and stored securely.

2. **Be Consistent**: Apply rules, discipline, and recognition evenly across your team to avoid the appearance of bias.

3. **Refer to HR Early**: When in doubt, escalate potential discrimination concerns to HR. Don't try to investigate or resolve it yourself.

4. **Avoid Vague Language**: Replace subjective terms like "bad attitude" with specific behaviors and impacts to ensure clarity and defensibility.

5. **Watch Your Reactions**: Avoid changing your demeanor or tone after someone makes a complaint; it can unintentionally appear retaliatory.

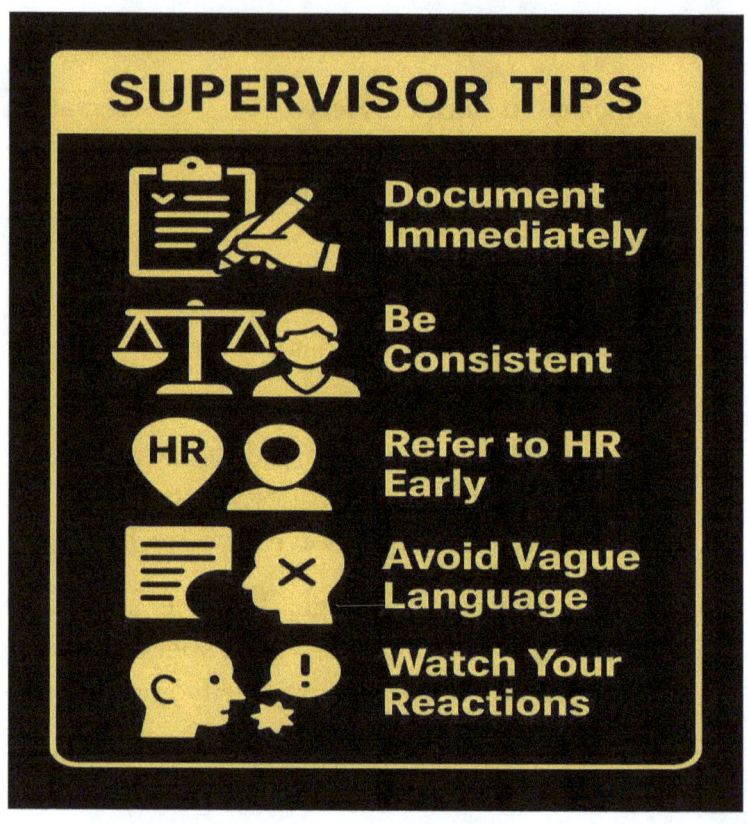

Figure 8. Supervisor Tip: EEOC *(original illustration created by Shelly Bell)*.

Case Studies Activities:

Case Study 1: Age Discrimination Overlooked

Scenario: Marcus, a 62-year-old technician with a strong performance history, was consistently passed over for upskilling and certification courses. His younger colleagues received those opportunities without request.

What EEOC Violation:

EEOC Violation: Age Discrimination under ADEA.

Possible Supervisor Misstep: Assuming Marcus wasn't interested or capable without asking. No documentation or rotation criteria were in place.

Corrective Action: The Supervisor implemented a transparent development opportunity calendar and consulted HR on inclusive practices.

Activities

Scenarios

Use these in training, discussion circles, or assessments.

Scenario 1: The "Culture Fit" Dilemma

You are interviewing two candidates. One is well-qualified but very different from your current team in communication style and background. A peer suggests going with the "better culture fit."

What do you do?

_____
_____
_____
_____
_____

What questions should you ask yourself about bias?

___

How do you ensure your hiring decision is EEOC-compliant?

___

Scenario 2: The Pregnancy Comment

An employee tells you she's pregnant. During a team meeting, you jokingly say, "Looks like someone's about to take a long vacation!" She later seems distant and misses work. HR informs you that a complaint has been made.

What did you do wrong?

___

How could a seemingly harmless comment turn into a discrimination issue?

_____
_____
_____

_____

Figure 9. Discrimination Pregnancy *(original illustration created by Shelly Bell).*

Quick Guide: Supervisor EEOC Compliance Checklist

Do

- Treat all employees consistently.
- Document all performance conversations.
- Refer discrimination concerns to HR immediately.
- Use objective criteria for promotions, hiring, and evaluations.
- Provide requested accommodations through HR guidance.

Don't

- Joke about age, disability, pregnancy, or race
- Retaliate—subtly or overtly—against an employee who files a complaint.
- Delay documentation until things escalate.
- Investigate or resolve complaints alone.
- Use "gut feelings" to justify employment decisions.

Avoid these costly compliance missteps:

(This may appear in a table version for the paper or hard copy version)

What NOT to Do	Why It's a Problem
Assume intent doesn't matter	EEOC evaluates **impact**, not just intent. "I didn't mean to offend" isn't a defense.
Delay or avoid documentation	Lack of written records weakens your position and increases legal vulnerability.
Handle discrimination complaints alone	You must **escalate to HR** — never investigate or resolve complaints by yourself.
Use subjective labels like "not a fit"	These vague justifications are red flags in EEOC reviews if not clearly defined.
Retaliate subtly	Even shifting someone's duties or tone after a complaint can be seen as retaliation.
Make jokes about protected traits	Humor related to race, age, gender, or disability can become grounds for claims.

Notes:

Figure 10. Creating a workplace of Respect *(original illustration created by Shelly Bell)*.

Part 2: Creating a Workplace of Respect

As a supervisor, you set the tone for how employees treat each other and how they experience the workplace. Policies and laws matter, but what truly shapes a company's culture is how those rules are applied in daily interactions. That's why your role in preventing discrimination and harassment isn't just about following the law—it's about building a respectful, inclusive environment where employees can thrive.

In this part of the book, we'll focus on two of the most critical responsibilities you carry: **Anti-Discrimination** and **Anti-Harassment**.

- **Anti-Discrimination** laws protect employees from unfair treatment based on race, color, religion, sex, national origin, age, disability, or genetic information. These protections extend to hiring, promotions, discipline, pay, and other conditions of employment. Your awareness and decisions directly affect whether employees feel valued and treated equitably.

- **Anti-harassment** policies and laws ensure that all employees can work in an environment free from unwanted conduct that creates a hostile or intimidating atmosphere. This includes sexual harassment, bullying, and other inappropriate behaviors. As a supervisor, you're often the first person to hear about these issues—and your response can either resolve the problem or allow it to escalate.

From an HR Manager's perspective, I've seen supervisors underestimate the influence they have in preventing these problems. Small actions—choosing words carefully, addressing inappropriate jokes immediately, or treating every concern seriously—can prevent larger issues down the road. On the other hand, failing to address discrimination or harassment quickly and effectively can lead to legal claims, damaged morale, and the loss of good employees.

In this section, we'll break down the laws and policies into straightforward, actionable steps. You'll learn how to recognize both obvious and subtle signs of discrimination and harassment, document incidents correctly, and respond in ways that protect both employees and the organization. We'll also discuss how to build a team culture that discourages inappropriate behavior from the start.

Supervisors who master these skills aren't just following the rules; they're creating a workplace where employees feel safe, respected, and able to focus on their work. This not only reduces legal risks, it improves productivity, retention, and trust in leadership.

By the time you finish this section, you'll know how to identify, address, and prevent discrimination and harassment with confidence. You'll understand your legal obligations, your role in shaping workplace culture, and the steps you can take to lead a team where respect isn't just a policy, it's a daily practice.

Chapter Four Bridging the Gap Understanding Anti-Harassment

*"Culture is the behavior you reward and the behavior you tolerate." – **Reed Hastings***

Introduction: Your Role as a Supervisor

As a supervisor, you are the gatekeeper of workplace culture. Whether you've been in your leadership role for decades or are just starting out, it's critical that you recognize that harassment has no place in your organization. More than just following rules, your behavior sets the tone for your entire team. One misstep—or a failure to act—can have legal consequences, damage employee morale, and seriously hurt your leadership credibility.

75% of workplace harassment victims experience retaliation when they speak up. — Equal Employment Opportunity Commission (2024)

What Is Workplace Harassment?

Harassment in the workplace refers to any unwelcome conduct based on race, color, religion, sex (including sexual orientation, gender identity, or pregnancy), national origin, age (40 or older), disability, or genetic information. This behavior becomes unlawful when enduring it becomes a condition of continued employment or when it creates a work environment that a reasonable person would consider intimidating, hostile, or abusive (EEOC, 2023).

As a supervisor, you must understand that it's not about your intent—it's about how your words and actions are received. Even what may seem like harmless teasing, nicknames, or jokes can deeply impact someone and result in legal action. If a person feels targeted, unsafe, or marginalized because of your actions or the behavior of someone on your team—and you fail to address it, you may be held accountable.

Harassment is not always obvious. Sometimes it's subtle. It can be a pattern of behavior or a serious one-time incident. That's why your role includes being alert and aware, listening carefully to concerns, and addressing behaviors swiftly. If you ignore a complaint or fail to act on something you witness, your inaction could be interpreted as complicity.

"What you permit, you promote." – **Unknown**

Subtle Signals of Tolerance

You may not think of yourself as someone **who would tolerate harassment**—but tolerance isn't always obvious. It shows up when a supervisor laughs at an off-color joke rather than addressing it, or when inappropriate comments are brushed off as 'just how they are.' These are not harmless moments. They are signals to your team that bad behavior will go unchecked. And when people feel unsafe or unsupported, trust in leadership is lost.

It's essential to remember that harassment doesn't need to happen in front of you for you to be responsible. If someone on your team is harassing a colleague—even if it's through texts, social media, or whispering in the break room—you are still accountable if you know or should have known it was happening and did nothing. The Equal Employment Opportunity Commission (EEOC) holds employers and their agents, including supervisors, liable for failing to take action when harassment occurs.

1 in 4 employees witnessed workplace harassment in the past year, yet only 35% reported it. — SHRM (2022)
Source: SHRM Harassment Prevention Strategies

Creating a Culture of Safety

Don't wait for someone to come forward with a formal complaint. Many employees don't speak up because they fear retaliation, they worry they won't be believed, or they assume nothing will happen. That's why you need to create a culture where people feel safe sharing concerns. During meetings or one-on-ones, invite feedback. Make it clear you want to know if something feels off. And most importantly—when someone does speak up—believe them, support them, and take immediate steps.

> *"In the end, we will remember not the words of our enemies, but the silence of our friends."*
>
> *– Martin Luther King Jr.*

The Cost of Mishandling Complaints

Handling complaints the wrong way can have devastating consequences. If you downplay the issue, suggest the person is overreacting, or fail to report it properly to HR, you put the organization at risk of lawsuits and regulatory investigations. But even more critically, you put your own leadership position in jeopardy. In today's workplace, ignorance of policy is not a defense. As a supervisor, you are expected to know the rules and to act decisively.

You must also think about the message your silence sends to others. When an employee sees a peer harassed and nothing happens, it tells them they might be next. It tells them they're not protected. And that's the beginning of a toxic culture—one that affects morale, retention, and even productivity. A disengaged team is the natural outcome of poor supervision.

Harassment is not a problem that solves itself. Hoping it 'blows over' or 'works itself out' is both dangerous and irresponsible. You must take action. That includes documenting the situation, escalating to human resources, and following through on next steps. If you've witnessed behavior that could be harassment and you choose not to document or report it, you become part of the problem.

Workplace bullying and harassment cost U.S. businesses an estimated $22 billion annually in lost productivity, turnover, and legal costs. — Workplace Bullying Institute (2021)

Leadership and Workplace Integrity

Leadership is not just about driving results—it's about protecting people. You are not just a supervisor of work; you are a steward of workplace integrity. That means standing up for others, setting the standard for how people treat one another, and eliminating any behavior that undermines respect, equity, or safety.

This responsibility can feel heavy at times, but it is non-negotiable. Being proactive doesn't mean being confrontational. It means setting expectations early, reinforcing them often, and showing through your actions that your team's well-being matters. You can foster a culture where people feel empowered to speak up, confident in their protections, and proud of the workplace they're a part of.

*"A leader is one who knows the way, goes the way, and shows the way." – **John C. Maxwell***

Why Harassment Has No Place in Your Organization

Harassment isn't just a policy violation, it's a direct threat to your team's sense of safety, your organization's culture, and your personal credibility as a leader. Every supervisor must treat harassment as a **zero-tolerance** issue. There is no middle ground. Employees will look to you to set and enforce standards. If you don't act, you're silently endorsing the behavior.

Your Legal and Ethical Responsibilities

Supervisors have an obligation to protect employees from harassment under federal laws such as **Title VII of the Civil Rights Act of 1964, the Americans with Disabilities Act (ADA),** and state-specific anti-harassment statutes. As outlined in the **EEOC's 2024 Enforcement Guidance on Harassment**, employers and their agents (including supervisors) may be held liable if they knew or should have known about harassment and failed to address it appropriately (EEOC, 2024).

You are not expected to investigate complaints—that responsibility lies with HR—but you are required to report any concerns immediately. This legal responsibility also extends to maintaining confidentiality and protecting the individual from retaliation.

What Happens When Complaints Are Ignored

Failing to report or mishandling a harassment complaint can have consequences for both you and the organization. According to the Society for Human Resource Management (2022), supervisors who downplay or dismiss complaints often contribute to higher turnover, reduced employee engagement, and reputational damage. In some cases, supervisors may face disciplinary action or termination for failing to fulfill their duty to report.

A report from the Equal Rights Advocates (2021) also emphasizes that mishandled complaints increase the risk of litigation. When a pattern of tolerance or inconsistent enforcement exists, it can be used in court to prove willful neglect of employee protections.

Organizations with strong anti-harassment training and policies saw a 43% reduction in EEOC complaints over a five-year span. — U.S. Department of Labor (2023)

Lead with Integrity

Effective leadership requires courage, awareness, and consistency. You must lead by example—challenging inappropriate remarks, correcting disrespectful behavior, and reinforcing your organization's zero-tolerance stance. Employees should never wonder where you stand on harassment. Your actions must reflect a firm, visible commitment to respect and safety.

Key Takeaway: Your Role in Ending Workplace Harassment

As a supervisor, you are the front line of protection when it comes to workplace respect and psychological safety. Harassment doesn't start in policy manuals—it starts in behaviors. And it ends when leaders like you take firm, consistent action to prevent it.

You don't have to be perfect—but you do have to be proactive. Your job is to listen, to act, and to create an environment where every employee knows they're safe, valued, and heard. This means setting expectations early, modeling inclusive behavior, addressing problems immediately, and partnering with HR without hesitation.

Harassment has no place in any organization. And when you take that seriously—not just in words but in actions—you protect more than just your company from legal risks. You protect people. You build trust. You shape a team that thrives on respect, not fear.

Remember: every decision you make, every comment you overlook, and every behavior you confront sends a message. Choose to lead with integrity, courage, and consistency. Your example is what defines your team's culture, make it one worth following.

Glossary Term	Definition
Harassment	Unwelcome conduct that creates a hostile, intimidating, or offensive work environment based on protected characteristics.
Protected Class	Groups of people legally protected from discrimination and harassment (e.g., race, sex, religion, age, disability).
Hostile Work Environment	A workplace where conduct interferes with an individual's ability to perform their job due to severe or pervasive harassment.
Retaliation	Adverse actions taken against an employee for reporting harassment or participating in an investigation.
Zero-Tolerance Policy	A strict policy approach that imposes automatic consequences for harassment or related misconduct.

Understanding terminology is vital when creating an environment of trust in the workplace. This is in no way all the terms you should know, but it is a starting point for your journey on this topic.

Supervisor Tips

1. **Act Promptly** – Don't wait. If you witness or hear about harassment, act immediately and follow protocol.

2. **Document Everything** – Keep detailed notes on what occurred, when, who was involved, and what steps were taken.

3. **Stay Neutral, But Serious** – Avoid bias or assumptions when hearing complaints. Treat all reports with respect and seriousness.

4. **Model Respect** – Demonstrate inclusive language and behavior daily. Supervisors set the tone.

5. **Partner with HR** – You're not alone. Use your HR team as a resource and refer any questionable behavior immediately.

Case Studies

Activities:

Case Study 1: The Joke That Went Too Far

Sandra is a new supervisor on the warehouse floor. A long-tenured employee, Tom, often makes jokes referencing female co-workers' appearances. When Sandra hears one of these comments during a team meeting, she nervously laughs along but does not report it. A month later, an employee files a complaint, and the investigation shows multiple team members were uncomfortable for months. Sandra is disciplined for failing to address the behavior and receives mandatory retraining on harassment prevention.

What is the lesson that Sandra should have taken from this experience?

_____
_____
_____
_____

Lesson: Silence can be perceived as approval. Even non-verbal responses like laughing can undermine the credibility of a leader.

Activities

Scenario 1: Off-Handed Comments in a Breakroom

You overhear two employees laughing about a meme on someone's phone that references a stereotype. Another team member nearby seems uncomfortable but doesn't say anything about the incident that occurred.

What should you do immediately, and how should you follow up?

_____
_____
_____
_____
_____

Scenario 2: Misusing "Intent" as a Defense

An employee comes to you with a concern about another teammate who repeatedly comments on their clothing and appearance. When you address it, the accused responds, "I didn't mean anything by it—it was a compliment!"

What's your next step, and how do you ensure that the employee feels heard and protected?

_____
_____

Quick Guide: Supervisor's Role in Preventing Harassment

Action	Description
Model Respectful Behavior	Demonstrate inclusive, professional conduct every day.
Set Expectations Early	Reinforce zero-tolerance during onboarding and team meetings.
Intervene Promptly	Don't ignore or delay action when issues arise.
Report Immediately	Contact HR or follow internal procedures without making assumptions.
Document Objectively	Keep detailed, unbiased records of what was reported and how you responded.
Avoid Retaliation	Do not change assignments, schedules, or treatment of complainants.
Support the Complainant	Ensure they feel safe, heard, and protected throughout the process.
Maintain Confidentiality	Share details only with those who need to know.
Follow Up Respectfully	Check in to ensure the concern was addressed and the employee feels supported.
Stay Trained	Regularly review policies and refresh your harassment prevention knowledge.

What Not to Do (Supervisor Pitfalls)

Don't...	Why It's a Problem
Ignore complaints or "brush them off"	Sends a message that harassment is tolerated.
Make excuses for behavior (e.g., "They didn't mean it")	Undermines the experience of the complainant and damages trust.
Fail to document incidents	Lacks a record for HR or legal follow-up; could be seen as negligence.
Promise confidentiality you can't guarantee	Legal processes may require disclosure—misleading employees increases risk.
Retaliate or allow retaliation	It is illegal and can lead to serious consequences, including lawsuits.
Delay reporting to HR	The longer the delay, the greater the risk to the employee and the organization.
Address harassment informally without HR	Reduces accountability and may escalate liability.
Use humor or sarcasm when discussing harassment	Minimizes the seriousness and creates discomfort or confusion.
Involve others who don't need to know	Breaches confidentiality and could be considered gossip or retaliation.
Assume the issue is resolved without following up	Leaves employees feeling unsupported and may damage retention and morale.

Notes:

Chapter Five Anti-Discrimination

"Fairness does not mean everyone gets the same. Fairness means everyone gets what they need." – **Rick Riordan**

Introduction: Your Role as a Supervisor

Discrimination is not always loud, obvious, or intentional—but its impact can be deeply harmful and legally serious. As a supervisor, you play a key role in identifying, preventing, and correcting discriminatory behavior. Your leadership directly affects how inclusive, fair, and legally compliant your team culture becomes. If employees experience unequal treatment and you fail to intervene or act, your credibility—and the organization's—can quickly unravel.

In 2023, the EEOC received over 67,000 charges of workplace discrimination.— EEOC Charge Statistics, 2024

What Is Workplace Discrimination?

Workplace discrimination occurs when an employee or candidate is treated unfavorably because of characteristics protected under federal law—such as race, color, religion, sex (including sexual orientation and gender identity), national origin, age (40 or older), disability, or genetic information. This includes bias in hiring, promotions, discipline, job assignments, or terminations (EEOC, 2024). Discrimination may be overt or subtle, and it is your responsibility to recognize both.

"Diversity is being invited to the party. Inclusion is being asked to dance." – **Verna Myers**

Recognizing Bias in Everyday Actions

Discrimination doesn't always look like a slur or an outright denial of opportunity. It can manifest as exclusion from growth projects, assigning less desirable shifts, applying harsher discipline inconsistently, or failing to recognize performance. Supervisors must reflect: Who gets the chance to lead? Who's left out of meetings or mentorship? Patterns speak volumes—even when no one is explicitly complaining.

How Supervisors Can Prevent Discrimination

You have the power to prevent discrimination by practicing fairness in decision-making, documenting performance, questioning assumptions, and consulting HR before making personnel decisions. Proactively fostering inclusion—such as ensuring all voices are heard in meetings and rotating development opportunities—is not just good leadership; it's essential risk mitigation.

> "If you're not intentionally including, you're unintentionally excluding." – **Joe Gerstandt**

The Risk of Inaction

Failing to address discrimination can result in **Equal Employment Opportunity Commission (EEOC)** claims, lawsuits, reputational harm, and loss of employee trust. Inconsistent decision-making is one of the leading causes of unintentional discrimination. Don't rely on gut instinct or 'how things have always been done.' Use consistent, policy-aligned processes for evaluating performance and making employment decisions.

Organizations with diverse leadership teams are 36% more likely to outperform peers financially. — McKinsey & Company, 2020

Lead with Equity and Accountability

Being fair isn't always easy—it requires intention, self-awareness, and courage. If you're unsure about a decision's fairness, pause and **consult.** Inclusion must be an ongoing effort that's embedded in your leadership approach. Your team is **watching** to see if opportunities, praise, and accountability are handed out fairly. If you want respect, you must first give it— **equally.**

"Injustice anywhere is a threat to justice everywhere." – **Martin Luther King Jr.**

Recognizing Subtle Discrimination

Not all discrimination is intentional or malicious. Often, it's embedded in unconscious bias, outdated practices, or assumptions about who **'fits'** a role. For example, consistently assigning administrative tasks to female employees, overlooking older workers for tech projects, or offering advancement opportunities only to those who mirror existing leadership—can all be signs of discriminatory behavior.

Supervisor's Accountability

Supervisors are not just responsible for their own conduct—they are accountable for the climate they allow. If you see favoritism, if your decisions disproportionately affect certain groups, or if patterns of underrepresentation emerge and go unaddressed, you may be enabling discrimination. Your silence or failure to act sends a message that this behavior is acceptable, even if unintentional.

"Equity is the pathway to equality." – **Gloria Ladson-Billings**

Discrimination and Legal Risk

In 2023, the Equal Employment Opportunity Commission (EEOC) reported over **67,000** charges of workplace discrimination.

Discrimination related to race, sex, disability, and retaliation consistently ranks among the top categories (EEOC, 2024). While the organization may ultimately be held liable, supervisors who fail to report or correct violations can face internal disciplinary action, damage to their reputation, or demotion.

Employees who feel included are 42% less likely to look for another job. — Deloitte, Global Human Capital Trends Report, 2021

Building Inclusive Practices

Inclusion is not just about compliance—it's about creating a workplace where all employees can succeed. This means soliciting diverse perspectives, removing barriers to advancement, and ensuring accountability in your own decision-making. Ask yourself regularly: *Am I treating all team members with equity, regardless of their background or identity?* Inclusion doesn't happen passively. It must be actively reinforced.

More than 55% of employees report experiencing or witnessing discrimination in the workplace. — Catalyst, 2022

Key Takeaway: Build the Culture You Want to Lead

Discrimination doesn't just impact **individuals**—it chips away at your entire team's unity, trust, and momentum. When someone feels excluded, unfairly judged, or overlooked because of who they are, it creates invisible walls. These walls divide teams, reduce collaboration, and undermine the confidence employees have in you as a leader.

As a supervisor, you have an opportunity—one that many others in the organization do not. You interact with employees daily. You see the real culture, not just the posters or policy handbooks. You witness how people are treated, who gets praised, who is invited to meetings, and who is left behind. That visibility makes you powerful. But with that power comes a choice: you can reinforce bias by ignoring it—or you can challenge it, reshape it, and create something better.

Building an inclusive, non-discriminatory culture doesn't require a major announcement or a new policy initiative. It starts with small, intentional decisions. It's how you assign work, who you mentor, how you give feedback, and whether you speak up when someone is being dismissed or stereotyped. These everyday actions become your team's norms. They become your legacy.

Don't wait for HR to fix cultural problems. Don't assume someone else will speak up. You are the leader. That means your behavior gives permission—to be fair, to be courageous, or to turn a blind eye. Make your choice clear. Be vocal about your commitment to fairness. Encourage open dialogue. And be willing to admit when your own habits need adjusting—because that's what strong, growth-minded leaders do.

Discrimination has no place on **high-performing** teams. When decisions are rooted in **equity**—

based on skill, effort, and potential—employees notice.

Morale rises. Trust deepens. Innovation increases. You retain top talent, and you build the kind of workplace others want to be part of.

This is your moment to lead with integrity. Be the kind of leader who sets the standard—not because you were told to, but because you know it's what your team deserves.

Glossary Term	Definition
Discrimination	Unfair or unequal treatment of individuals based on protected characteristics such as race, gender, age, or disability.
Implicit Bias	Unconscious attitudes or stereotypes that affect understanding, actions, and decisions.
Protected Class	A group of people legally protected from employment discrimination under federal law.
Equity	Ensuring fair treatment, access, opportunity, and advancement for all people.
Inclusion	The practice of creating environments in which any individual or group can feel welcomed, respected, supported, and valued.

Workplace discrimination is forever changing. As a supervisor it is up to you to address any issues that may arise related to discrimination. Don't allow uncomfortable situations to stop you from being a great supervisor.

Supervisor Tips

1. **Review Your Decisions for Bias** – Ask yourself: Would I make the same decision if this employee had a different background?

2. **Rotate Opportunities** – Don't always give stretch assignments or visibility to the same people. Share the growth.

3. **Use Standardized Evaluation Criteria** – Apply the same performance expectations and feedback process to all employees.

4. **Address Exclusion** – Speak up if you notice someone being left out of conversations, mentorships, or recognition.

5. **Consult HR Before Major Personnel Actions** – Always involve HR when dealing with discipline, promotion, or dismissal decisions

Figure 11. Supervisor Tip: Discrimination
(original illustration created by Shelly Bell).

Activities

Scenario 1: Promotion or Preference?

You're deciding between two employees for a team lead role. One has more experience, but the other shares similar personality traits with your leadership style. You feel more comfortable with the latter.

1. What would an equitable process look like in this decision?

_____
_____
_____
_____
_____

2. Who should you consult before proceeding?

_____
_____
_____
_____
_____

Scenario 2: Subtle Language in Feedback

You tell a high-performing woman of color on your team, "You're very articulate and professional—it's refreshing." She becomes distant afterward.

1. Could your feedback have been received as biased or offensive? Why?

_____
_____
_____
_____
_____

2. How can you check yourself and repair trust?

_____
_____
_____
_____
_____
_____
_____

Quick Guide: Supervisor's Role in Preventing Discrimination

Action	Description
Treat Fairness as a Standard	Use consistent methods for evaluation, discipline, and recognition.
Be Aware of Patterns	Look for recurring imbalances in promotions, assignments, or feedback.
Involve HR Proactively	Don't wait until an issue escalates. Seek guidance early.
Speak Up Early	Address microaggressions or favoritism even when no formal complaint is made.
Document Objectively	Record the rationale for decisions involving hiring, discipline, and promotion.
Check Your Blind Spots	Engage in training and self-reflection to uncover unconscious bias.
Champion Inclusive Culture	Normalize inclusion by rotating visibility, mentorship, and leadership roles.
Follow Policy	Align decisions with your organization's anti-discrimination and EEO policies.
Encourage Reporting	Let employees know they can come to you with concerns without fear of retaliation.
Lead with Intention	Your leadership defines what is tolerated—set the tone purposefully.

What Not to Do (Supervisor Pitfalls)

Don't...	Why It's a Problem
Assume equality = fairness	Treating everyone the same ignores different needs, experiences, and barriers.
Make hiring decisions based on a "gut feeling"	This invites unconscious bias and lacks objective evaluation criteria.
Ignore patterns in assignments or promotions	Repeatedly favoring certain individuals can indicate discrimination—even if unintentional.
Avoid difficult conversations about bias	Silence allows exclusion and discrimination to persist.
Dismiss employee concerns as "too sensitive"	Invalidating feedback damages trust and shows a lack of empathy.
Use coded language in feedback	Terms like "not a culture fit" or "too emotional" can reflect biased perceptions.
Fail to document decisions	Without clear documentation, your judgment may appear arbitrary or discriminatory.
Over-rely on one employee's input	Relying on one trusted team member's perspective without a broader insight can lead to favoritism.
Assume bias training is enough	Training without action changes nothing. Leadership behavior must align with expectations.

Don't...	Why It's a Problem
Exclude HR when unsure	Bypassing HR increases the risk of poor or inconsistent decisions and legal exposure.

Figure 12. Supervisor Pitfalls: Discrimination *(original illustration created by Shelly Bell).*

Notes:

Figure 13. : Supervisor Role Safety First *(original illustration created by Shelly Bell).*

Part 3: Safety First – Your Role in a Compliant Workplace

As a supervisor, one of your most important responsibilities is keeping your team safe. Production goals, deadlines, and daily challenges may shift, but safety is non-negotiable. A safe workplace doesn't just **happen**—it's the result of consistent leadership, clear communication, and strict adherence to **safety laws and standards.**

In this part of the book, we'll focus on **Safety and OSHA compliance**—two areas where your leadership has a direct impact on employee well-being and the organization's legal standing.

- **Safety** isn't just about wearing protective gear or following posted rules; it's about building a culture where every employee looks out for one another and understands that safety is part of the job, not an afterthought.

- **OSHA (Occupational Safety and Health Administration)** regulations set the minimum standards for workplace safety. These rules are designed to prevent accidents, illnesses, and injuries on the job—and as a supervisor, you're responsible for ensuring your team understands and follows them.

From an HR Manager's perspective, I can tell you that safety failures are rarely the result of one big incident—they're often the outcome of small oversights that add up over time. A cluttered work area, a missed inspection, or an ignored near-miss report can set the stage for accidents that harm employees and cost the organization in fines, lost productivity, and a damaged reputation.

This section will walk you through your role in OSHA compliance and everyday safety leadership. You'll learn how to recognize hazards, respond to incidents, conduct inspections, and promote safety practices that become second nature for your team. We'll also cover how to document safety measures, handle OSHA inspections, and address violations quickly and effectively.

Supervisors who lead with a safety-first mindset don't just reduce accidents—they increase trust and morale. Employees are more engaged when they know their leaders genuinely care about their well-being, and compliance becomes easier when safety is treated as a shared responsibility.

By the end of this section, you'll have the knowledge and tools to meet OSHA standards, prevent workplace injuries, and lead your team in a way that prioritizes safety without slowing productivity. You'll be equipped to create a workplace where employees go home each day in the **same—or better—condition** than when they arrived.

Chapter 6 Safety – Protecting Your People and Your Workplace

"An ounce of prevention is worth a pound of cure." – **Benjamin Franklin**

As a supervisor, you are the messenger of safety. Your actions, decisions, and example directly influence how your team approaches hazards, follows procedures, and values safety in their daily work environment.

In my HR and supervisor roles, safety has always been a top concern. I have seen firsthand the devastating impact of workplace accidents—not just on the injured employee, but on their coworkers, the unit, and the organization as a whole. If you've ever had an employee severely injured or even die at your facility, it is something you will never forget. Over my career, I have experienced both. Those moments reinforced my belief that supervisors must embrace their role and responsibility in safety—not as an afterthought, but as a daily, visible priority and sincere.

Safety is not only about compliance with OSHA or avoiding fines. It is about protecting lives, building trust, and creating an environment where every employee feels confident that they will go home in the same condition they arrived.

Understanding Your Role in Safety

Supervisors are the bridge between policy and practice. You implement the procedures, enforce the rules, and model the behaviors that define your organization's safety culture.

According to *The Supervisor's Safety Toolkit* (NSC Press, 2020), 94% of employees say they are more likely to follow safety rules when they see their supervisor doing the same. This means if you take shortcuts, so will your team. When you correct unsafe behavior, your team learns that safety is non-negotiable.

Legal and Compliance Responsibilities

Workplace safety laws are primarily governed by the *Occupational Safety and Health Administration (OSHA)*. OSHA's general duty clause requires that employers provide a workplace "free from recognized hazards that are causing or are likely to cause death or serious physical harm" (Occupational Safety & Health Review Commission, 2022).

Your responsibility as a supervisor includes:

- Identifying hazards and removing or mitigating them.
- Enforcing the use of required personal protective equipment (PPE).
- Ensuring that safety training is completed, understood, and documented.
- Following Lockout/Tagout (LOTO) and other critical procedures without exception.
- Reporting incidents, near misses, and unsafe conditions immediately.

Failing to act can have serious legal consequences—not just for the company. As a supervisor, you can potentially be held personally liable if negligence is proven. Negligence is something that most supervisors don't even consider to be part of the scope of their position.

Hazard Recognition and Prevention

One of your most important safety tools is your eyes. Every walk through your area is an opportunity to spot hazards: a frayed extension cord, a missing machine guard, missing PPE and unmarked wet floor.

Safety Leadership (Roughton & Crutchfield, 2021) emphasizes that hazard recognition must be proactive. Don't wait for an accident to occur. Use daily safety walks and encourage your team to report hazards and near-misses without fear of punishment.

Building a Safety Culture

A strong safety culture is more than rules—it's a shared belief that everyone is responsible for safety. Research shows that companies with strong safety cultures have 48% fewer incidents and 20% higher employee engagement (National Safety Council, 2022).

Ways to build safety culture:

- Lead daily toolbox talks that are relevant and interactive.
- Recognize employees who demonstrate proactive safety behaviors.
- Follow through on every safety concern raised.
- Celebrate safety milestones, such as "X days without a recordable injury."

Training and Communication

Training isn't "one and done." Skills fade, bad habits creep in, and procedures change. The National Institute for Occupational Safety and Health (*NIOSH* 2020) recommends regular refresher training, hands-on demonstrations, and interactive Q&A sessions to keep safety knowledge fresh.

As a supervisor, you should:

- Verify certifications are current (forklift, confined space, etc.).
- Provide hands-on instruction, not just policy reviews.
- Use downtime for quick safety quizzes or scenario discussions.

Your Personal Leadership Moment

I'll never forget the first time I had to notify a family that their loved one was not coming home. It was the result of a preventable incident—a bypassed safety guard to save a few seconds. In that moment, I realized that every safety decision I made—or ignored—had life-changing consequences for someone. That memory drives me to never walk past a hazard without taking action.

As a supervisor, you will face production pressures, conflicting priorities, and employees who push boundaries. Your job is to protect them—even if it means stopping work. Safety is never negotiable.

Responding When an Incident Occurs

When an incident happens:
1. Ensure immediate medical care and secure the

scene.
2. Report the incident to HR and safety personnel.
3. Document facts objectively—what happened, when, where, and who was involved.
4. Participate in root cause analysis to prevent recurrence.

Your role is not to assign blame; rather, it is to uncover and address the underlying causes. You have a team that will help you to address any actions that may need to be taken.

So, take care of your people.

Final Thoughts:

Safety as a Leadership Commitment

As a supervisor, your role in safety extends far beyond compliance checklists and regulatory requirements. You are the daily embodiment of your organization's safety culture. Every action you take, from wearing your own PPE to addressing unsafe behaviors, signals to your team what truly matters.

Safety leadership is about consistency, visibility, and courage—consistency in applying standards, visibility in being present on the floor, and courage to stop work or challenge unsafe practices, even under pressure. These traits protect not only your employees' physical well-being but their trust in you as a leader.

Never underestimate the ripple effect your decisions

have. A single hazard corrected today might prevent a tragedy tomorrow. Conversely, a shortcut allowed today might lead to a lifetime of regret. Lead with the mindset that safety is not optional—it's the foundation for everything else your team achieves.

Remember: Every employee deserves to go home safe, every single day. Your leadership makes that possible.

Glossary Term	Definition
PPE (Personal Protective Equipment)	Gear such as gloves, safety glasses, helmets, and earplugs designed to protect against hazards.
LOTO (Lockout/Tagout)	A safety procedure ensuring machines are properly shut off and not restarted before maintenance or servicing is complete.
Near Miss	An unplanned event that did not result in injury but had the potential to cause harm.
Hazard	Any source of potential harm or adverse health effect on people.
Safety Culture	The shared values, beliefs, and behaviors that determine how safety is prioritized in the workplace.
Incident Rate	A standardized measure of workplace injuries and illnesses within a given period.
Root Cause Analysis	A method of identifying the underlying reasons for why an incident occurred to prevent recurrence.
Ergonomics	The science of designing the workplace to fit the worker, reducing strain and injury risk.
Job Safety Analysis (JSA)	A process that breaks down a job into steps, identifies hazards, and determines safe ways to perform each step.

These definitions only represent a small part of the key terms that will be used in your role as a supervisor. However, they are vital to understand.

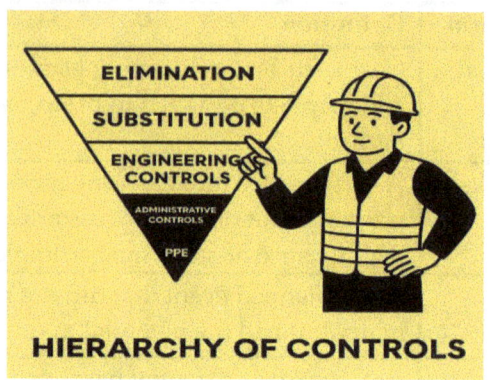

Figure 14. Hierarchy of Safety (*original illustration created by Shelly Bell*).

Supervisor Tip

Treat near misses as seriously as actual incidents. They are warnings you can't afford to ignore. Investigating them now may prevent a tragedy later.

Figure 15. Supervisor Tip Safety (*original illustration created by Shelly Bell*)

Case Study

The Missed Lockout

During the night shift, a technician began cleaning a machine without performing Lockout/Tagout. The supervisor assumed the team knew the procedure and didn't verify compliance. Minutes later, another worker unknowingly activated the machine. Luckily, no one was injured—but it was a near-fatal incident.

What was the lesson in this case study?

_____
_____
_____
_____
_____

Lesson: Never assume training has been understood. Personally verify compliance.

Activity:

Safety Scenario Triggers

- You see an experienced operator bypass a guard to save time.

- A new-hire reports that a ladder feels 'wobbly' but says it's been that way for years.

- You notice several employees not wearing the required hearing protection in a high-noise area.

Scenario with Supervisor Response

Scenario: An employee quietly tells you about a leaking chemical container but says they didn't report it because 'we're already short-staffed.'

What You Should Say:
"Thank you for letting me know. This is important, and we need to address it immediately. Safety always comes first. I'll get this reported and taken care of right away."

Figure 16. Thank you for Reporting (*original illustration created by Shelly Bell*).

Safety Quick Guide

- Conduct daily safety walks.
- Verify PPE compliance.
- Follow up on hazards immediately.
- Document training and incidents.
- Recognize safe behaviors publicly.

What Not to Do

- Don't walk past hazards without action.
- Don't assume employees know procedures.
- Don't downplay near misses.
- Don't skip PPE because 'it's just a quick task.'

Figure 17. What Not to Do Safety *(original illustration created by Shelly Bell).*

Notes:

Chapter 7 OSHA – Understanding Your Role in Workplace Compliance

"By failing to prepare, you are preparing to fail."

– Benjamin Franklin

When the word OSHA comes up in the workplace, many supervisors feel an immediate wave of anxiety. For some, it conjures images of inspectors arriving unannounced, clipboards in hand, looking for violations. I remember my first interaction with an OSHA representative—it was surprisingly pleasant. Why? Because I was prepared. I had every document ready, I understood my role, and my team knew theirs. That preparation turned what could have been a stressful event into a professional and cooperative exchange.

This is why it's so important for supervisors to understand their role when interacting with OSHA. It's not a matter of if you will have an OSHA-related situation, it's a matter of when. And the better prepared you are, the smoother it will go. In my years in HR, I've seen that this is often a weak point for supervisors, regardless of how long they've been in their roles. Let's fix that.

Workplace injuries and illnesses cost U.S. employers $167 billion annually (OSHA).

What is OSHA and Why Supervisors Should Care

The Occupational Safety and Health Administration (OSHA) is a federal agency created to ensure safe and healthy working conditions by enforcing standards and providing training, outreach, education, and assistance. While OSHA holds employers accountable, the day-to-day actions that make compliance a reality are carried out by supervisors.

Data Point: OSHA reports that workplace injuries and illnesses cost U.S. employers over $167 billion annually, factoring in lost wages, medical costs, and productivity loss.

Your role isn't just about avoiding citations—it's about protecting people, preserving productivity, and safeguarding the organization's reputation. Every action you take—or fail to take—can either keep your team safe or put them at risk.

Your Legal and Compliance Responsibilities

Under OSHA's General Duty Clause, every employer must furnish "a place of employment free from recognized hazards that are causing or likely to cause death or serious physical harm."

For supervisors, this translates to:

- Knowing the OSHA standards that apply to your work area.
- Ensuring employees are trained on applicable hazards and procedures.
- Monitoring compliance on a daily basis.
- Documenting safety training, incidents, and corrective actions.

Statistic: Only 35% of supervisors feel fully confident in responding to an OSHA inspection (ASSE Supervisor Preparedness Survey, 2023). That means nearly two-thirds of supervisors are unprepared for an event that could happen tomorrow.

Data Point: Repeat OSHA violations can result in penalties exceeding $156,259 per violation (OSHA, 2024), up 45% from five years ago due to penalty inflation adjustments.

Why you need to know this: As a supervisor, you are often the first line of defense when it comes to preventing OSHA violations. If you don't understand the legal requirements, you could unintentionally put your team and the company at risk. Not knowing the law isn't a defense—OSHA will hold the organization accountable, and your leadership decisions will be under scrutiny.

Top OSHA Citation Areas You Must Know

Each year, OSHA publishes its Top 10 Most Frequently Cited Standards. Understanding these areas helps you focus on the highest-risk issues:

1. Fall Protection – Over 7,000 citations in FY2023.

2. Hazard Communication – Incomplete or outdated safety data sheets.

3. LOTO (Lockout/Tagout) – Failure to control hazardous energy.

4. Respiratory Protection – Missing fit tests or improper respirator use.

5. Scaffolding – Unsafe design or assembly.

6. Powered Industrial Trucks – Lack of operator certification.

7. Machine Guarding – Missing or bypassed guards.

8. Fall Protection – Training – Insufficient training records.

9. Eye and Face Protection – Failure to enforce PPE use.

10. Ladders – Damaged or improperly used equipment.

Data Point: In 2023, over 60% of total OSHA citations fell into these ten categories.

Why you need to know this: These aren't just 'OSHA priorities'—they are the most common hazards your team could face daily. If you can identify and address these issues before OSHA does, you not only reduce the risk of citations but also prevent injuries that can change someone's life forever.

Documentation: Your First Line of Defense

During an inspection, documentation is often the first thing an OSHA officer will request. Training sign-ins, incident reports, safety audits, near-miss logs, and equipment inspection records all play a role.

Statistic: Supervisors who maintain organized documentation reduce citation risk by over 40% compared to those who rely on ad-hoc records (NSC Workplace Safety Study, 2022).

Data Point: The average OSHA inspection lasts 3 to 5 days for manufacturing facilities—meaning your recordkeeping system must be 'inspection-ready' at all times.

Why you need to know this: When OSHA comes calling, your documentation is often your proof that you've done your job. If it's missing, incomplete, or outdated, it will be assumed you didn't act. Proper records protect you, your team, and the company — and they show OSHA that safety is part of your culture, not an afterthought.

Proper LOTO procedures prevent approximately 120 deaths each year (OSHA).

LOTO – A High-Stakes Procedure

Lockout/Tagout (LOTO) violations have ranked in OSHA's Top 10 citations for over two decades. This procedure prevents the accidental startup of machinery during servicing and is critical to preventing severe injuries.

Statistic: OSHA estimates that proper LOTO procedures prevent approximately 120 fatalities and 50,000 injuries each year.

Supervisors must:
- Ensure only trained and authorized personnel perform LOTO.
- Post written procedures at each machine.
- Conduct refresher training at least annually.
- Enforce immediate corrective action for non-compliance.

Why you need to know this: Lockout/Tagout is one of the most critical safety procedures you will oversee. If it's ignored or done incorrectly, the consequences are often severe—sometimes fatal. As a supervisor, you have the authority to stop unsafe practices and the responsibility to make sure every person on your team understands and follows LOTO procedures.

Preparing for an OSHA Inspection

You can't control when OSHA shows up, but you can control how prepared you are:
- **Have a point of contact** – Designate who will guide the inspector.
- **Organize documents** – Training records, hazard assessments, injury logs.
- **Conduct mock inspections** – Identify and correct issues before the real thing.
- **Train your team** – Everyone should know what to do if approached by an inspector.
- **Be professional and honest** – If you don't know the answer, say so and get it.

Companies that perform quarterly self-audits experience 26% fewer OSHA citations (BLS Workplace Safety Review, 2023).

Why you need to know this: An inspection isn't the time to figure things out, it's the time to show that your team is always ready. The way you prepare now determines whether an OSHA visit is a quick confirmation of compliance or a long, stressful process with serious consequences.

Incident Response and Reporting

When something goes wrong:

- Secure the area and care for injured employees.
- Notify Safety and HR immediately.
- Document everything factually—avoid speculation.
- Cooperate fully with OSHA if an investigation is required.

Statistics: OSHA requires that fatalities be reported within 8 hours, and in-patient hospitalizations, amputations, or loss of an eye within 24 hours.

Why you need to know this: The moments after an incident are when your leadership matters most. OSHA will look at how you responded—whether you acted quickly, documented properly, and followed procedures. Your actions in these moments can protect your team, your company, and your own credibility as a leader.

Quarterly self-audits reduce citations by 26% (BLS, 2023).

Final Thoughts: OSHA as a Partnership, not a Punishment

Too many supervisors hear the word "OSHA" and immediately tense up, as if it's the workplace equivalent of a traffic cop waiting to hand out tickets. But here's the truth—OSHA's mission is to ensure safe and healthy working conditions for every worker in America. That mission is not in conflict with yours. In fact, it's directly aligned.

Your role as a supervisor is to create an environment where safety is so ingrained in your team's habits that an OSHA inspection isn't a threat—it's simply another set of trained eyes helping you confirm that your hard work is paying off. When you operate this way, compliance is not an occasional scramble before a visit; it's a standard you live out every single day.

Think about it: OSHA provides the framework, resources, and standards, but you bring those rules to life. You're the one translating regulations into daily practices—whether it's ensuring PPE is worn, verifying Lockout/Tagout steps are followed, or reinforcing hazard reporting. You set the tone that safety is everyone's job, not just that of the safety manager.

When an inspector walks in, your documentation, training records, and clean work areas speak louder than any speech you could give. If you've been leading consistently—conducting safety walks, responding to near misses, and updating your team on hazards—there won't be any panic, just professional confidence.

Yes, inspections can feel stressful – but remember: OSHA can also be a powerful resource. They offer training materials, industry-specific safety data, and even voluntary consultation programs that identify hazards before they result in citations. Treating OSHA as a partner means you actively seek those resources, learn from their feedback, and apply their best practices.

If you're new to supervision, this mindset will save you from falling into the trap of reactive safety management. If you're a veteran leader, it will help you keep safety fresh and evolving. Either way, the goal isn't to "beat" OSHA—it's to create such a strong culture of safety that their visits become opportunities for improvement and acknowledgment rather than moments of fear.

When you and OSHA are on the same side, inspections become just another day on the job—because every day, your team is already working to the standard they expect.

Glossary Term	Definition
OSHA	Occupational Safety and Health Administration, the federal agency responsible for workplace safety regulations.
General Duty Clause	The OSHA requirement that employers maintain a workplace free from recognized hazards.
Citation	A formal notice from OSHA of a safety or health violation.
PPE	Personal Protective Equipment used to minimize exposure to hazards.
LOTO	Lockout/Tagout is a safety procedure to ensure machines are properly shut off before maintenance.
Hazard Communication	OSHA standard ensuring information about chemical hazards is provided to workers.
Incident Report	Documentation of details related to a workplace injury, illness, or near miss.
Self-Audit	An internal review to identify safety hazards before OSHA inspections.

Recordkeeping	Maintaining OSHA-required logs and documents of workplace injuries and training.
Abatement	Correction of safety hazards identified by OSHA.

As a supervisor, understanding the terminology that is used when an incident happens can help during a stressful time. It will also work to put your employees at ease. Because you have the situation under control.

Supervisors Tips

- Always lead safety meetings with real examples from your workplace.

- Perform daily walk-throughs to spot hazards before they cause harm.

- Keep your documentation 'inspection-ready' at all times.

- Address unsafe behaviors immediately — never wait for an incident.

- Build a safety-first culture by recognizing and rewarding safe behavior.

Figure 18. Safety and OSHA (*original illustration created by Shelly Bell*).

Case Studies

Case Study 1: During an unannounced OSHA inspection, a manufacturing supervisor's preparation and organized documentation reduced what could have been multiple citations to just a single minor correction.

_____
_____
_____
_____
_____

Case Study 2: A supervisor ignored repeated warnings about faulty ladder equipment. An employee's fall led to a serious injury and a $70,000 OSHA fine — plus significant damage to team morale.

_____
_____
_____
_____
_____

Scenarios

Scenario 1: An OSHA inspector arrives unexpectedly at your site. How do you respond?

_____
_____
_____

Scenario 2: You discover an employee working without PPE in a high-risk area. What steps do you immediately take?

Figure 19. PPE Compliance (*original illustration created by Shelly Bell*).

Quick Guide: OSHA Readiness

Figure 20. Quick Guide OSHA Readiness *(original illustration created by Shelly Bell).*

- Know your applicable OSHA standards.
- Maintain organized and current documentation.
- Train your team regularly on hazard awareness.
- Perform quarterly self-audits.
- Establish clear inspection protocols.

What Not to Do

- **Don't** ignore hazards because 'we've always done it this way.'

- **Don't** wait until after an incident to update safety procedures.

- **Don't** hide information from OSHA inspectors.

- **Don't** allow untrained employees to perform high-risk tasks.

- **Don't** neglect regular equipment inspections.

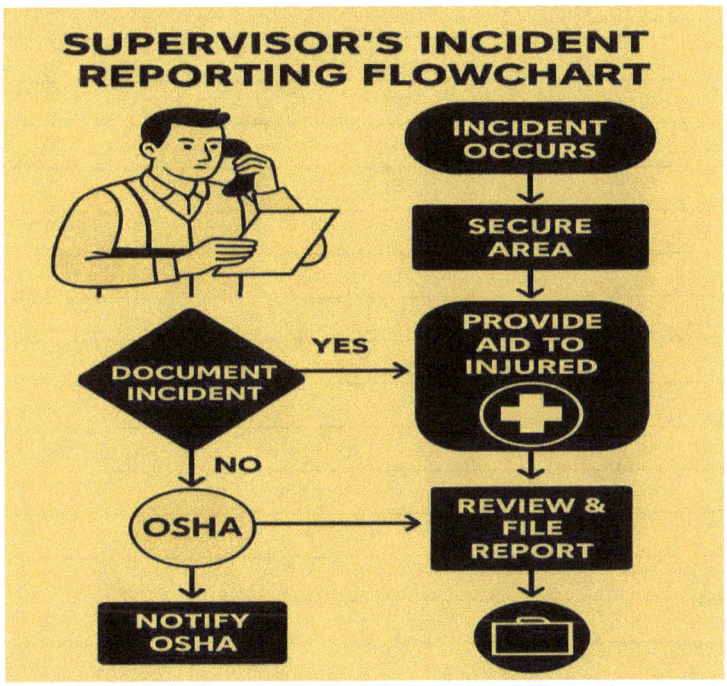

Figure 21. Supervisor Incident Flowchart (*original illustration created by Shelly Bell*).

Notes:

COMING NEXT IN THE EWI SUPERVISOR'S SKILLS SERIES

UP NEXT:

BOOK 2 – BUILDING HIGH-PERFORMANCE TEAMS
Unlock strategies to mspire, engage, and retain top talent— while tackling real-world team challenges head-on.

BOOK 3 – MASTERING CONFLICT & COMMUNICATION
Gain the tools to handle tough conversations, resolve work-place disputes, and become a confident communicator in any situation

BOOK 4 – LEADING THROUGH CHANGE
Navigate change with resilience and purpose—because great leaders don't just adapt, they lead the way forward

BOOK 5 – THE SUPERVISOR'S TOOLBOX
Your go-to guide for HR essentials, forms, checklists, and tips to keep you compliant, organized, and effective

STAY CONNECTED

FOLLOW US ON FACEBOOK
thesupervisorshrfix

GREAT SUPERVISORS NEVER STOP LEARNING— THIS SERIES IS YOUR ROADMAP TO BECOMING THE LEADER EVERYONE WANTS TO FOLLOW.

Figure 22. Elevate Within Series Recap *(original illustration created by Shelly Bell)*.

Your Journey as a Supervisor Continues

You've just completed *Book 1* of the Supervisor Track series, and with it, you've taken an important step toward becoming a confident, legally-aware, and people-focused leader. By working through **FMLA, FLSA, EEOC, Anti-Discrimination, Anti-Harassment, and Safety/OSHA compliance**, you've built the legal and ethical foundation every supervisor needs.

From here, your ability to lead within the law will guide every decision you make—ensuring fairness, building trust, and protecting your employees, your organization, and yourself. You now have tools to handle leave requests with confidence, apply wage and hour rules correctly, address workplace concerns quickly, and foster a respectful and safe environment for your team.

But leadership doesn't stop here. This book is just one part of a larger journey designed to support you in every aspect of supervision. The *Supervisor HR Fix* series was created to give you a complete leadership toolbox—one that grows with you as your responsibilities evolve.

- **Book 2** focuses on the front end of the employee lifecycle—*Conducting Effective Interviews and Onboarding New Hires, Basic Compensation and Pay Practices*, and *Retention Basics*. You'll learn how to hire the right people, bring them into the team smoothly, and keep them engaged for the long term.

- **Book 3** dives into performance management—*Conflict Resolution, Managing Attendance, Progressive Discipline*, and *Giving Feedback and Coaching Performance*. You'll master the skills to guide, correct, and inspire your team.

- **Book 4** builds your leadership presence—*Emotional Intelligence, Creating a Positive and Respectful Team Culture, Handling Complaints, Building Accountability*, and *Managing Diversity and Inclusion*. These are the people-focused skills that transform good supervisors into great leaders.

Every book in this series is practical, plain-spoken, and built from real-world HR and leadership experience. Each one connects to the next, creating a comprehensive guide to leading teams effectively, legally, and with integrity.

If you found value in this book, I encourage you to continue your learning journey with the rest of the series. The more tools you have, the more prepared you'll be for the challenges and opportunities of leadership.

Remember—supervision is not just a job; it's a responsibility that directly shapes the success of your team and your organization. Keep building your skills, keep asking questions, and keep striving to lead in a way that inspires trust and respect.

Your next chapter as a leader is waiting. Let's keep going.

References

Budd, J. W. (2020). *Human resources law* (8th ed.). Cengage Learning.

Burr, SHRM-SCP, Matthew W and Hamilton-Gill, FCIPD, Sarah (April 20, 2023). The Evolving World of Human Resource Consulting https://www.shrm.org/topics-tools/news/organizational-employee-development/evolving-world-human-resource-consulting

Brassel, Sheila, PhD, Shaffer, Emily, PhD &Travis Dnika J, PhD; Catalyst. (2022). Emotional tax and work teams: A view from 5 countries https://www.catalyst.org/insights/2022/emotional-tax-teams

Church, A. Y. (2019). *Fundamentals of safety management*. Safety Press.

Compliance Place. (2023). *Supervisors: The key to safety program success*.

Department of Labor. (2019). DOL issues latest pronouncements on the FMLA and FLSA. *Holland & Knight*. https://www.hklaw.com/en/insights/publications/2019/03/dol-issues-latest-pronouncements-on-the-fmla-and-flsa

Equal Employment Opportunity Commission. (2024). Charge statistics (charges filed with EEOC). https://www.eeoc.gov/sites/default/files/2025-

02/Table E1a. Charge Receipts by Basis or Statute %28All Statutes%29 FY 1997 - FY 2024.xlsx

Equal Employment Opportunity Commission. (2024). Enforcement guidance on harassment in the workplace. https://www.eeoc.gov/laws/guidance/enforcement-guidance-harassment-workplace

Equal Rights Advocates. (2025). Ending harassment and retaliation at work. https://www.equalrights.org/issue/economic-workplace-equality/

Hammer, L. B., et al. (2019). A training intervention for supervisors to support work-life policy. *PMC*. https://www.ncbi.nlm.nih.gov/pmc/articles/PMC3791083/

Hammer, L. B., Kossek, E. E., Anger, W. K., Bodner, T., & Zimmerman, K. L. (2019). A training intervention for supervisors to support work-life policy. *National Center for Biotechnology Information*. https://www.ncbi.nlm.nih.gov/pmc/articles/PMC3791083/

Harvard Business Review. (2019). How to reduce bias in your hiring process.https://hbr.org/2019/06/how-to-reduce-personal-bias-when-hiring

Hunton Andrews Kurth LLP. (2024). The unwitting 'employer': Individuals liable for FLSA violations. https://www.hunton.com/insights/publications/the-unwitting-employer-individuals-who-may-be-liable-for-flsa-violations

Krieg DeVault. (2024). Adapting performance metrics for FMLA and approved leave. https://www.kriegdevault.com/insights/adapting-performance-metrics-for-employees-on-reduced-schedules-for-fmla-and-other-approved-leave

Loafman, M., Strickland, K., & Ruiz, A. (2024). *Harmonizing federal anti-discrimination laws*. Cornell Law School. https://community.lawschool.cornell.edu/wp-content/uploads/2024/09/Loafman-et-al.-final-1.pdf

National Employment Law Project. (2021). *Retaliation trends in U.S. workplaces*.

National Safety Council. (2022). *Toolbox talks and safety outcomes*.

NIOSH. (2020). *Hazard communication training for supervisors*.

NSC Press. (2020). *The supervisor's safety toolkit*. National Safety Council.

Occupational Health & Safety Online. (2020). *The supervisor's crucial role in safety performance*. OH&S.

Occupational Safety & Health Review Commission. (2022). *OSHA compliance manual*.

Pérez, S., Martínez-Córcoles, M., & Díaz-Cabrera, D. (2022). Supervisory integrity and safety climate: The role of 'walking the talk.' *Journal of Safety Research, 80*, 27–39.

Ross, C. A. (2019). *Employment law for managers* (2nd ed.). McGraw-Hill.

Roughton, J., & Crutchfield, N. (2021). *Safety leadership* (2nd ed.). Elsevier.

Society for Human Resource Management. (2022). *Harassment prevention strategies*. https://www.shrm.org/resourcesandtools/hr-topics/behavioral-competencies/global-and-cultural-effectiveness/pages/harassment-prevention.aspx

Society for Human Resource Management. (2022). Harassment prevention strategies. https://www.shrm.org/topics-tools/news/inclusion-diversity/preventing-sexual-harassment-workplace#:~:text=%22A%20major%20element%20of%20this,on%20sexual%20harassment%20for%20employees

U.S. Department of Labor. (2022). *Strategic enforcement of the FLSA*. https://www.dol.gov

U.S. Department of Labor. (2023). *Family and Medical Leave Act*. https://www.dol.gov/agencies/whd/fmla

U.S. Department of Labor. (2023). *Fair Labor Standards Act compliance assistance*. https://www.dol.gov/agencies/whd/flsa

U.S. Equal Employment Opportunity Commission. (2023). Charge statistics FY 2023. https://www.eeoc.gov/data/enforcement-and-litigation-statistics-0

Index

Accommodation (ADA) See EEOC; FMLA & ADA overlap

Acknowledgments..14

Anti-Discrimination 71–84

Anti-Harassment......................................57–70

Breaks & meal periods 23–37

Case studies FMLA 7–22; FLSA 23–37; Harassment 57–70 Discrimination 71-84

Child labor (FLSA) 23–37

Classification (exempt vs. non-exempt)..........23–37

Conclusion..117–118

Documentation......................23–37; 38–53; 57–84

EEOC (equal employment opportunity) 38–53

Eligible employee (FMLA) 7–22

Equivalent position (FMLA) 7–22

Family member (FMLA)................................7–22

FLSA (wage & hour)................................23–37

FMLA (leave) 7–22

Harassment (workplace) 57–70

Hostile work environment........................57–70

In loco parentis (FMLA) 7–22

Incapacity (FMLA) 7–22

Inclusion/Equity......................................71–84

Introduction 1–3

Job protection/reinstatement (FMLA)............7–22

Leave (FMLA) — qualifying reasons 7–22

LOTO (lockout/tagout) 88–116

Microaggressions / subtle bias............38–53; 57–84

OSHA 101–116

Overtime (FLSA) 23–37

PPE (personal protective equipment) 88–116

Protected classes.............................38–53; 57–84

Quick guides & checklists 7–22; 23–37; 38–53; 57–70

References ....119+

Retaliation 38–53; 57–70

Return-to-work (FMLA)..............................7–22

Safety (general).......................................88–100

Serious health condition (FMLA) 7–22

Supervisor tips ....Throughout

Timekeeping (FLSA) 23–37

Twelve-month period (FMLA) 7–22

What not to do 7–22; 23–37; 38–53; 57–84

Your journey as a supervisor (series roadmap) ... 117+

Acknowledgments

I would like to extend my heartfelt gratitude to Annie Preston for her invaluable support with editing, proofreading, and reference checks. Her guidance and dedication played a vital role in helping me bring this dream to life. I am deeply appreciative of her contributions and the encouragement she has given me along the way.

A special note of thanks for the cover design and illustration, which was created in collaboration with digital tools (DALL-E, ChatGPT Versions 4, 4o and 5) based on my original concept, vision, and branding. This design reflects the heart of the book and the mission behind HRUNeed/Elevate Within.

About the Author

Shelly Bell, MBA, SHRM-CP, is a seasoned Operations and Human Resources leader with over two decades of experience spanning manufacturing, retail, nonprofit, and education sectors. She has partnered with executives, business owners, and community leaders to design and implement strategies that drive employee engagement, strengthen compliance, and foster inclusive workplace cultures.

As Founder and CEO of **HRUNeed, LLC**, Shelly has developed and delivered workforce training programs—both in English and Spanish—serving diverse industries across multiple states. Her expertise covers recruitment, succession planning, employee relations, compensation strategy, safety management, and HR compliance. She has successfully led initiatives resulting in multi-million-dollar cost savings, significant reductions in turnover, and measurable boosts in employee engagement.

Shelly holds a Master of Business Administration in Human Resource Management and a Bachelor of Science in Business in Sustainable Enterprise from the University of Phoenix, as well as certifications in SHRM-CP, Project Management, and Diversity, Inclusion, and Equity. She has collaborated with notable HR and business leaders throughout her career, as well as in her work as a SHRM Certification Instructor.

Residing in Kentucky, Shelly is a proud partner, mother, grandmother, sister, and aunt. She is deeply committed to community service, volunteering with Feeding America, the United Way, and local youth programs. She also serves in leadership roles with the Chamber of Commerce and other civic organizations.

This is her first published book. To learn more about her work, visit www.HRUNeed.com and https://www.linkedin.com/in/shelly-bell

Figure 23. Thank you for Reading *(original illustration created by Shelly Bell)*.

The **HR Fix Series** is part of the **Elevate Within Professional Series**. Elevate Within is a movement designed to support the growth and development of leadership teams.

The Supervisor's Series contains four books created to guide supervisors at every stage of their career — whether newly promoted or experienced in their role. Each book provides supervisors with practical information on key HR topics that directly connect to their responsibilities.

Together, these books serve as valuable tools in the **Supervisor's Toolbox**, accompanied by activities at the end of each chapter to reinforce learning. Supervisors are encouraged to apply, the information throughout the series. **Please note that compliance-related content may change due to updates in state and federal laws or regulations.** It is your responsibility to stay informed of these changes and understand how they impact compliance issues that may arise during your career. Supervisors will find the books both relatable and easy to read. The supervisor's series is designed to be thought provoking and is best used alongside the **Participant's Guide**, which includes group activities to support team training and development.

Other Books in Series

Book 1: HR Compliance

Book 2: Front End Life Cycle

Book 3: Inspiring the Team Concept.

Book 4: Leadership Presence

www.ingramcontent.com/pod-product-compliance
Lightning Source LLC
Chambersburg PA
CBHW051941160426
43198CB00013B/2253